YOUR
MOVE,
GOD

YOUR
MOVE,
GOD

by
Sister Francis Clare, SSND

New Leaf Press
P.O. BOX 311, GREEN FOREST, AR 72638

Cover design: Sister Josephe Marie Flynn SSND
Layout design: Sister Gilmary Lemberg, SSND
Photography: Sister Glenna Carroll, O.P.

First Printing, April 1982
Second Printing, October 1982 (Revised Edition)
Third Printing, June 1983
Fourth Printing, March 1985
Fifth Printing, December 1986

Library of Congress Catalog Number: 82-081212
International Standard Book Number: 0-89221-102-4

TABLE OF CONTENTS

Dedication
Acknowledgments
Foreword
Preface

Chapter

DEDICATION

This book is lovingly dedicated to all who call God their Father.

ACKNOWLEDGMENT

I wish to express appreciation to Father Armand Nigro, S.J., and Sister Justin and Father John Wirth for being my "prophets to discern the prophet";

to Sister Paul Terese, member of our Provincial team; Sister Paula Young, Sister Therese Even, Beverly Hodgins, and Marge Freking for reading and refining the manuscript;

to Carla Brey and Jeanne Frietag for time spent typing;

to countless readers of WOW, GOD for their encouragement and prayerful support;

to Wilma and Clair Hutchins for their home in Pinellas Park, Florida, where I spent two months listening to God;

and most of all, to our God "for from Him and through Him and to Him are all things. To Him be the glory forever."

FOREWORD

The God of Abraham, Isaac and Jacob is the Father of our Lord, Jesus Christ, and continually communicates with us, revealing His preferences and gracious purposes.

Prophets are people who prayerfully listen to God and share with us what they hear. The God of the Hebrew and Christian scriptures reveals Himself and His provident concerns through the prophets who left us these sacred writings. That same God continues to speak to us in our times, through people like Sister Francis Clare.

This collection of love-notes is for us all. We are invited to read them in the prayerful way in which they were heard and written.

Father Armand Nigro, S.J.
Professor of Religious Studies
Gonzaga University
Spokane, Washington 99258

PREFACE

We have arrived in the game of life at a stalemate where no one can make a significant world-changing move—except a deeper move of surrender to the Living God, as we say; it is YOUR MOVE, GOD!

Knowing the mess humanity is in, we need no analyzing of the bad news. What we are eager for is the GOOD NEWS.

> "God is doing a sovereign work! We cannot program it. We cannot halt it. We can say, 'Do it, God! Do it!' We can move when He says, 'Move!' We can praise God for what we see happening!"

Seven years ago when I wrote that in the concluding chapter of *Wow God*, it was both fact and prophetic utterance. It is still both fact and prophetic utterance.

I believe that God is ready to speak to all of us children about the mighty, irresistible love in the Father's heart, about His readiness for an unprecedented sovereign move of His Holy Spirit. I spent some sixty days away from the human scene to hear and now to share what God spoke to me for you. It comes from the heart and hand of the Father spoken to the heart and mind of a child.

This is not a book to be read in one sitting or even several sittings, but one to be savored and to bear fruit for many a season.

There are days when it seems you are on the mountaintop and there are days when you are in the pits (valley). It doesn't really matter whether it is in the mountaintop or the valley, as long as you yield to My work in you.

"Some people see the things that are and say WHY? I see the things that are not and say WHY NOT!" RFK quoted Shaw in a political sense. I quote and raise Shaw's question in a spiritual sense.

Why wouldn't the Father, the sovereign ruler of the universe, our Creator God, do a godly thing, an incredible thing when His almighty love and His omnipotent promises call for it?

Why wouldn't He make of the weakest and neediest of us a whole new creation when we turn to Him in conversion?

Why wouldn't He heal the centuries of "roots" in our psyche, no matter how bad our Humpty Dumpty is falling apart?

Why wouldn't He who created us recreate the wonderful work of His hands?

Why wouldn't our Father share with us His dominion over the elements, when He brought us who were willing into Kingdom-living?

Why wouldn't He do whatever needs to be done as we pray—It's **YOUR MOVE, GOD!**

My child,
    The words that I am giving to you
      are not just words to you
        but words for all My people.
    The work I am doing in you
      is not just a work that I would do in you alone
        but I would do it in all My people.
I will complete in them
    what I am completing in you.
I am their Father even as I am your Father.
I have called you apart to receive this word
    that you may proclaim it.

The needs that I see in you
   I see in them.
      The hunger
         the thirst
            the emptiness
               the brokenness
                  the need for purification and judgment
   I see in all of My people.
Even as I effect wholeness in you
   I will effect wholeness in them.

   You are on your way to a banquet feast of your God.
   You are walking into the very presence of your Father.
I have made you beautiful
   and I continue to make you beautiful.
I prepare you
   as I prepared Esther to meet the King.
The communion banquet I will give you is a new intimacy
   with your Father,
   an intimacy until now you have but tasted.
But now I will give you that intimacy in deep drafts.
            As you grow in this
I will clothe you in the strength and beauty of Jesus
            His splendor
            His prayer life
            His position before the Father.

   Fear not
      for I have readied you.
   All things are right.
   You will taste of the banquet
      and walk in the strength of it for many days.

There are days when it seems you are on the mountaintop
            and there are days when you are "in the pits."
        It doesn't really matter whether it is
                the mountaintop or the valley
                    as long as
                you yield to My work in you.
        There are things I do in the valley
        that I do not do on the mountaintop.

        There are things I effect in the depths of your spirit
                only when you come to rest in the valley.
    So be content with the valleys.
    When it seems there is nothing going on
                    and you long for the days
                    when I was so real on the mountaintop,
                    know that I am just as real in the valley.
    My work is just as real in the valley.
    My presence is just as real in the valley.
    It may take more faith to believe,
        but that is the time to exercise faith.
    Ask that I deepen your faith in My love.
    As the Spirit revealed Jesus to you,
            Jesus will reveal the Father to you
                    as you rest.[1] *

My child,
You will never fully know what it means
        to be an adopted child of your heavenly Father;
    you can only gain deeper and deeper insight into it.
Even now everything I have belongs to you.
As you enter from death into life
    all that I have will be yours forever.

*See FOOTNOTES page 144

My child, ponder the riches
            ponder the life
            ponder the meaning of belonging to Me and
you will never know what it means to be alone or lonesome.
Your roots are in a Father
    Who is Sovereign Ruler of the universe.

You ask: "How can I get to know You, my Father?"
    By living in My presence
        by living in My Word
            by allowing Me to live in you
                and you in Me.
Look at Jesus' life.
    How did He get to know His Father?
By spending time with Me
    by reverencing all the things I created
    by serving Me in brothers and sisters
    by coming daily to the mountaintop to seek My face.
Like you, Jesus grew in the knowledge of who He was
    and who I AM.
By My Spirit He was taught.
By My Spirit you will come to know your Father.

Let go of fear
    let go of apprehension for the future.
You have a Father who owns the cattle on a thousand hills. [2]
Every bird, everything that moves in the fields is Mine.
You need not
    dare not be anxious for tomorrow.
Your Father who cares for every sparrow that falls
    has care for you.
I am still the Great I AM.
I not only care
    I have power.
To Me the whole world is like
        a grain of sand that tips the scales
        a drop of morning dew falling to the ground. [3]

I give you power to trust Me in new ways
              to yield your energy to My divine energy.
Let trust be your gift to Me.
Whoever trusts in Me inherits My holy mountain. [4]
Why care about earthy things
      if you own My holy mountain, the place to be with Me?

You seek.
You ask.
You cry for power to discern My plan for your life.
Continue to seek
        to ask
        to trust.
Do not be anxious and you shall know.
Is anything too hard for Me?
Is anything beyond My love or My power?
Then learn to trust and rejoice in your Father always.

    With delight I often heard My Son say
    "I do not speak on My own
        it is the Father Who gives Me the words." [5]
    You too, My child, should be able to say
    The words that I speak are not my own
        it is the Father who gives me the words.
    When storms come up, you will be able to say
    It is my Father who allows the storm
                      the circumstance
                      the pruning.
    It will help you in difficulties to know
        it is your Father testing.
    Know that My power is sovereign
        and nothing can touch your life
            unless I allow it.
    Let Me hear you pray
        Father, if it be Your hand
            help me to accept it with all my heart.

My child,
I am mightily in love with you.
Let that love do all
        hold all together
        cast out all the works of the enemy
        cover all that is sin
        lead you in the way I would have you follow.
Keep your eyes on Me
    your spirit yielded to My plan
    your heart open to My love.
I will teach you to profit from all that comes into your life,
        the bitter
        the beautiful
        the surprises.

If only you would pay attention to Me
    your happiness would be like a river
  and your righteousness like the waves of the sea.[6]

How often you have been touched
    when someone has a grateful heart.
So it is with your Father.
There is never a time when you can thank Me too much
    for what I have done for you.
Have I not delivered you from the kingdom of darkness
    and transferred you into the Kingdom of Light? [7]
To realize what a miracle that is may take all eternity.
Begin now to thank Me
    for what you do not fully understand
    and do not fully see—
        your name written in the Book of Life
        your feet firm upon the Rock of Salvation.

With infinite intelligence
    I have honed you as My instrument.
I trust you, My child.
    Learn to trust Me, your Father.
I know what I am doing.
My plan to use you is right on course.
    You do not have to be ready by human standards.
    It is enough to be prepared by divine standards.
Fear not
    for the way I call you to walk.
No matter where you go
    or how high I take you
    you will find in the Word
        in the Name
        in the Blood of Jesus
            power
            strength and
            protection.

A faithful God has made a covenant with you.
Heaven and earth will pass away
but My Word to you shall not pass
without accomplishing what it says.[8]

My child,
I am content to bring you into My Divinity
through your humanity.
If it seems difficult at times
know that I understand.
I know what the human struggle is.
I know what is in the human heart.
But I also know how to change and
how to transform that heart.
Be content to be human.
I can work through your weakness
and *in spite of your sinfulness*
bring you into My holiness.

Jesus came to know Me on His mountaintop. You, too, will come to know Me on your mountaintop. For this reason I created you.

God, what is the biggest thing You are doing across the face of the earth? In your faith imagination see the question register on a heavenly computer screen. Its beam is being sent up from a meeting of theologians with questions like, "God, what are we going to do with what You are doing? What is the biggest thing You are doing? How can we do it with You?"

God: "The biggest thing happening across the face of the earth is the Holy Spirit is being poured forth for the renewing and the restoring of the Body of Christ for the glory of the Father."

That's it! Just that!

My child,
I will put a guard upon your eyes
    that they be blinded to the things
        that I would not have you see.
There are many things you no longer need to see
        or to be curious about;
    I, your God, am all you need.
Let go of those things you're tempted to see
                to hear
                to speak.
If the Father is not giving it to you, don't see it
             don't hear it
             don't speak it
             don't do it!
You can no longer mix the two kingdoms.

It is good sometimes to go in spirit
    to that place I am preparing for you
    to experience there My glory
            My light
            My peace
            My presence.

My Kingdom is more real
　　than the place where you live.
The heavens and the earth may pass away
　　but not the place I prepare for you.
Even though you find
　　　　beauty, goodness, and gifts around you
　　let your treasure be in your eternal home.
Let your heart be free from attachment to places
　　　　　　　　　　　　　　　to people
　　　　　　　　　　　　　　　to things.
The more you find your delight in Me
　　the more I will find My delight in you.

Like the shower of rain that just deluged from the sky
　　so the rain of My Spirit
　　　　is constantly being poured forth.
Absorb My Spirit
　　like a clump of dirt absorbs water.
　　　　It is Mine to give.
　　　　It is yours to receive.
　　　　To be human is to receive.
　　　　To be godly is to give.

It is no small thing that I am doing.
　　　　　　　It is a mighty thing.
It is an almighty thing that is happening.
It is happening because this is the day
　　　　　　　this is the hour
　　　　　　　this is the time
and you are among the chosen ones to work
　　　　　　　in this day
　　　　　　　in this hour
　　　　　　　in this time
　　　　　　　for the coming of My Kingdom.

As you freely seek My glory, My honor, My praise,
you can freely let go of all that would be your glory,
your honor and your praise. You shall have no need of
that because
>   you shall be clothed in My glory
>   you shall be filled with My praise
>   you shall know the honor of My honor.

Happy are the poor in spirit for theirs is the Kingdom.[9]
Yours is the Kingdom!
So let go of the things you still cling to
>   the things you are hoarding in your heart.

Let go!
Let Me be your God, your all, your fullest treasure.
It must be all for all!
>   That is a law in the Kingdom.

It gives me joy
>   to see the zeal that you have for the Kingdom
>   to see the desire that you have
>   >   to bring your brothers and sisters into a relationship
>   >   >   with their Father and with their Brother Jesus.

Know that I have given to you
>   the gift of evangelism
and I will increase in you that gift
>   if you ask Me
>   >   for I choose gladly to give you the Kingdom.[10]

>   Sometimes
>   it amuses Me to see the choices you make
>   the things you balance and weigh
>   in making those choices.
>   Like My servant, Paul
consider that nothing outweighs the choice
of continually knowing Jesus as Lord.[11]
>   When choices arise, ask yourself—
>   "Does this allow Jesus to be Lord?"

Love Me
    with your whole heart
        and
    I will fill your heart
        beyond anything you can imagine.
Love Me
    with your whole soul
        and
    I will fill your soul with joy
                        bliss, and
                        a radiance that you cannot imagine.
Love Me
    with your whole mind
        and
    I will transform it
        so the renewed mind in you
        will be the same as in Christ Jesus. [12]

Let everything you do be an act of worship
        your life poured out in gift to Me.
It is a gift from Me
        let it be a gift for Me.
In that holy house of Nazareth
        Jesus poured out His life in gift to Me
                moment by moment
                task by task
                day by day.
Jesus came to know Me on His mountaintop.
        You, too, will come to know Me on your mountaintop.
            For this reason I created you.
Prophets and kings desired to see what you see
                and did not see it;
            to hear what you hear
                but did not hear it. [13]

I have given wonders for your eyes to see
                         for your ears to hear
            that you might begin to know
               what the Kingdom of Heaven is like.

         Think of the most beautiful relationship
            any child has with a father.
         Think of the most extravagant dreams
            a father has for a child.
         You are that child and I am that Father.

It is not enough for you to think of what it means
      to belong to the Kingdom.
You must also take a look at what it means
      if you do not accept the Kingdom
      if your brother and sister
            do not accept the Kingdom
   what it means to be cast out
   what it means for all eternity
      to miss the love of your Father
      to miss the Kingdom that has been prepared
            for you from all eternity.
Have I not created you
      that you might live in My Kingdom now and forever!
My desire is for ALL to live in the Kingdom.

You have been rescued
      from the darkness and gloom of Satan's kingdom
            and brought into the Kingdom of My dear Son
      who bought your freedom with His Blood
            and forgave you all your sins. [14]

3

FAITHFUL GOD

I am delighted to see your faith growing from a
mustard seed into a mighty tree where others can
come and find shelter.

"The most I have is a tiny mustard seed of faith," a Chicago businessman complained to me. He had heard of God's Holy Spirit moving in other people's lives, other parishes, other churches, other dioceses.

Ted was in a place where nothing was happening except a grand exodus of people like himself, who had given up hope for their lives and their church.

"What God is doing is simple," I explained, "God asks that you say, 'Yes' to the two simple moves: first, to invite Jesus to be Lord of your life and your personal Savior; and second, to ask Jesus to baptize you in His Holy Spirit with all the manifestations of the Spirit. Our simple move is followed by God's sovereign move. The way you believe is the way you receive."

As we prayed with Ted through the two simple moves, I added, "Lord, show Ted in vision what You are doing."

God did. Ted saw the door of his heart open, a figure in white came in, the tiny, shiny object that was the mustard seed was on a table before him. To make conversation Ted simply said, "All I got is this tiny mustard seed." And he heard Jesus reply, "Stupid, why don't you plant it?"

That's all Ted needed to hear to surrender completely to the move of God's Spirit, the Father's love, Jesus' saving power. In minutes he was praying in tongues and minutes later he summed it up, "That's my kind of Man. If you are stupid, that's what you need to be called."

My child,
I have set My heart upon you.
As My chosen people found Me a faithful and provident God
    you will find Me a faithful and provident Father
        providing you with all that you need
           according to My riches. [15]

Even when you are not faithful
know that I am a faithful God
faithful to forgive when you repent
to be strong when you are weak
to be the one-hundred percent
when you feel like a zero.

I see in you the faith of a child
who believes the Father will keep all His promises.
That faith is My gift
like the faith I gave to Judith, to Esther,
to Mary, to Abraham, to Peter, to John.
I am delighted to see that faith growing
from a mustard seed into a mighty tree
where others can come and find shelter.
It is My delight to see growing within you
a living trust in the faithfulness of your God.
This is your gift to Me.

I call you in the early morning hour
for I, your Father, would speak to you.
Show Me your face and I will show you Mine.
Let Me hear your voice and you will hear Mine.
The cooing of the turtle dove is heard in the land.[16]
I have much to say to you.
Come then, My love, come.
Place your hand in the hand of My resurrected Son.
Feel the resurgence of the Resurrection power
healing
restoring
dispelling all that is darkness.

The mystery of the Resurrection is yours as it was Paul's.
You are being acted upon with the same Resurrection power.
Lift your head high.
Come walk with dancing feet.
Raise your hands in holy worship
in praise and delight before your God.
As you are a delight to Me
so I desire to be a delight to you.
Delight yourself in Me
and I will give you the desires of your heart.[17]

I ask that you be faithful to your promises.
Ask and I will give you the gift of faithfulness.
Continually return to your nothingness before Me
that I may be everything.
You cannot live in compromise.
You cannot live in separate compartments
with thoughts unlike My thoughts
with words unlike My words.
Let your aim be — All for All.

My child,
You look for security
I am your security.
You look for understanding
I am total understanding.
You look for peace
I am the fullness of peace.
I have begun a good work in you
and I will complete that work.
Reverence each new move of grace
each new revelation of My love
of My healing
of My using you and
you will come to know Who is working in you
and through you.

Keep yourself little
    and I will use you in big ways.
You have crossed your Rubicon. There is no going back.
There is only going forward into a deeper rest
    a deeper realization that you walk with your Lord
        that your hand is in the hand of your Father
        that He will guard you from harm.
All I have spoken to you, all I have promised
    I will do.
It is impossible for Me to go back on My Word.

Celebrate today My faithfulness in walking with you
    in the full power of My Spirit.
Even when you are unfaithful to Me
    My love and faithfulness are still there.
With My Father's love I await your return.
Like the Prodigal you wasted some of the goods
                            the graces
                            the light
                            the power I gave to you.

I, your loving Father, call you back
    not with reproach and condemnation
        but with infinite love.
As Hosea took back the prostitute, so I take back My children
    who have prostituted the graces
        and the blessings I have given them.
I take them back
    with a Father's heart
    with a Father's forgiveness
    with a Father's promise that though their sins be like
        scarlet they will be white as snow. [18]
I call back My children
    to robe them in righteousness
    to give them a ring for their finger
    to reinstall them in their Father's life and love.

My child,
I ask you to come into the Throne Room this night.
There your Beloved Bridegroom will pray over you
together with all the blessed.
We will pray
that your mind be open to see
what the Father shows you
that the anointing with the burning coal
that was upon Isaiah be upon you
that your lips speak the words I give you.
They are not from your heart, but from My heart.
They are not from your spirit, but from My Spirit.
They are not from your mind, but from My mind.
My Throne Room will be the place for your prayer these
weeks.
Come to it daily that I may empower you
and commission you
for all that I call you to do.

I see in you the desire to be faithful
and the fruit of faithfulness
even as I see the dry rot of infidelity.
I, the Divine Vinedresser,
will cut away the cause of dry rot
so you may be faithful to Me
as I am faithful to you.
I pour out upon your mind
your spirit
the circumstances of your life
a gift of fidelity to your Father's love.
You will be My faithful child
even as I am Yahweh, the faithful One.

4

BRIDE

This is the day when the Father will dance. He rejoices over you with gladness.

I learned a simple lesson from a woman who made possible the impossible. "Be it done according to Thy Word," was her response to God's move in her life; and the Word was made Flesh and dwelt among us. Today we say, "Blessed is she who believed what had been spoken to her by the Lord."[19]

God speaks a similar word to us and makes a familiar promise; "The Holy Spirit will come upon you." The need has never been greater for a personal Savior and an omniscient baptizer in the Holy Spirit.

The Spirit and bride say, "Come." Let all who hear answer, "I come." Let all who are thirsty drink of life-giving water without cost.[20]

Your life is Our life.
I, your Father, watch over it with you.
It is not a monstrous task We give you to live Our life.
It is Our task to keep your old life dead
        and to live Our new life.
Let Us have it.
Enter into that Hebrew rest
              pondering
              listening
              discerning
              resting.
Allow Us to initiate, to act, to arrange.
You have a Husband who would do for you all the lovely
    things a good husband would do for a bride.
You have a Father who loves you as He loves Jesus.
You have a Holy Spirit who has pledged to be your life.
You have a family of brothers and sisters cheering for you.
You are part of a vast army of Christians who have learned
    that the only thing worth living for
        and worth dying for
           is the Father's love.

Love My Son each day
  with the fresh love of a young bride
    who can trust her husband for anything.
Many of My children have become
  nothing but nagging old wives.
Examine the thoughts that race through your minds
  the words that come forth from your lips.
How many are bridal thoughts and words
  full of bridal trust and love?
Be for My Son a beautiful bride
  for that is what you are
    and what you will be for all eternity:
    bride of My Son
      who is the King of kings
        and the Lord of lords!

My child,
If you are to know Who I am and what I am doing
  look to Jesus, your divine Bridegroom, to teach you.
He will reveal to you the Father
  as He knows the Father.
You cannot achieve this.
Dispose yourself so that it can happen.

With the Spirit we are three in One.
Sometimes you look to One
  and then to Another to do a work.
We will teach you
  to allow your life to flow and to rest
    in what each of Us is doing within you.
There is much you need to learn
  that only Jesus can reveal to you
    of My love
    of My working
    of how I would use your humanity
  even as I used the humanity of Jesus.

Jesus was human like you.
He had to learn
to listen
to become.
Like Jesus you are called to learn
to listen
to become only what glorifies your
Father.
How well Jesus knew this.
How well I would teach you.
This is the only reason for all the signs and wonders
for all the miracles that follow you—
That your Father be glorified.

Being in the center of worship
is being in the center of the battle.
Jesus will fight for you and stand with you.
Stand with Him, as a beautiful young bride.
As I call you to be a bride, I call the whole church
to be formed into a beautiful, perfect, radiant bride.
I will have for My Son a victorious
faithful
loving
valiant bride
formed by My own hand
shaped on My own potter's wheel
redeemed by the Blood of My own Son
designed in the heart of your Father
from all eternity.

As a bridegroom rejoices over the bride
your God rejoices over you
your beauty
your goodness
your purity
all that He sees within you as His lovely bride.
Your Bridegroom rejoices and invites you to rejoice in His
joy.
He delights in who you are and where He has brought you
in the life He shares with you now
and the life He will spend with you for all eternity.
Most of all
He delights to see you love Him as your Beloved
to trust Him for every detail of your life
to see you do everything out of love
because He is the Beloved of your heart.

The hand of a Father and the hand of a Bridegroom guides
   you.
Your Father rejoices to send you as His evangelist
   washed in the Blood, clothed in His righteousness.
You say, "Can this be really real?"
Yes, My beloved, this is the reality of living in the Kingdom.
Mine is a Kingdom of joy and celebration.
I desire a bride that celebrates
                  that knows how to rejoice
                  that knows how to sing and how to dance.
I am a celebrating God!
I am a God of tremendous joy!
I call you to be a bride of tremendous joy
      that rises not just from your heart, your spirit, and your
         mind
         but from My heart, My Spirit, and My mind.
Rejoice in your Lord always,
      in all the circumstances of your life
      in what is difficult and what is easy
      when I am near and when I seem far away.
My joy is like a deep water spring within you.
When you are quiet before Me
      a spring of joy will well up within you.
Anything that robs you of your *peace,* your *joy* and your *love*
      is not from Me.
They are My gifts to you
      and no one shall take them from you.

See yourself hand-in-hand
    with your Bridegroom and your Creator.
Feel the radiance of Resurrection power
    flowing from Jesus' Hand into your life.
Feel the resurgence of Creative power
    flowing from your Father's Hand into your hand.
Remind yourself that all the beauty
                all the power
                all the energy of the entire universe
    has gone forth from the Hand that holds your hand.
All that people pay fortunes to buy
    all they travel the world to see
        came forth from the Hand
            in which you rest.

Each of you is called to be Jesus' personal bride
    and to be part of His corporate bride.
Have that love, respect, and openness for each other
    that I have for you.
To love Jesus and not be a living love
    a life-giving light for each other
        is impossible.
It is sin.
It blocks what I need to do.
Trust Jesus to be that perfect Bridegroom.
In turn you will be the perfect bride.

It is true you have found Him Whom your soul loves. [21]
Like the bride in the Song of Solomon
    hold Him and never let Him go.
Never exchange Him for the things of the world
    for ways you would walk
        and things that you would do apart from Him.
Never let Him go and you will find He will never let you go.
You will know the joy of belonging to Jesus
    the security of belonging to the King of kings
        in Whom all power is given in heaven and on earth.

Rest in that love, that security, and that power
and nothing shall harm you.
Jesus is the Beloved Bridegroom
who comes in the night to one who is waiting
with lamp trimmed and burning.
He has come many times and found your lamp burning.
He has rejoiced to find you waiting.
As you are waiting, We are waiting to take you
as Jesus' beloved bride into the Kingdom.

I call you, My child,
to see the sunrise with your Beloved
to greet the dawn with the psalms
as Jesus did in Galilee.
I call you to worship
and to sing the praises of your Father with Him.
The Lord reigns; let the earth rejoice.
The mountains melt like wax before the Lord.
All peoples have seen His glory.[22]

Jesus loves you today as He has loved you from all eternity
with the strong young love of a young Bridegroom.
He is ravished with your beauty
not unlike the beauty of His Father.
He sees none of your weaknesses as bad.
They are the very things that make you throw yourself on Him
as your Savior, your Bridegroom.
They are the very things that make you totally dependent on
Him
to be clothed with His love
His energy
His righteousness.

This is the day when the Father will dance
   and He rejoices over you with gladness.
      He renews you in His love.
      He sings joyfully because of you.[23]
Rejoice for what you have in Jesus.
Together you stand in veiled but real victory

   before your Father.
   You are two in one—*Bridegroom and bride*
      in the heart of your Father.

5

CALL

And you are,
breathe easy, My
child, but one small
part of a mammoth
movement of My
grace on earth.

The first commandment is to love the Lord your God with your whole heart, your whole soul, your whole mind and with all your strength.

Many of us have just been attempting to love God with our whole mind and it hasn't worked too well. The fruit of holiness, the power of evangelism, the signs and wonders just haven't been what we might have hoped for.

The Father encourages and chides us to a mighty surrender of where we are and what we are called to as we pray—"It's Your Move, God!"

My little child, in whom I am so big
   why do you worry as if it were all your work and not Mine?
I have set My hand upon you
   and under the powerful anointing of My hand
      you are seeing the magnitude of the task
      the glorious workings of My grace
      the desire of My heart to reach My broken, defeated ones
   but, at the same time and with the same grace
      you have become intensely aware of the smallness
                  the incapabilities
     even the sinfulness of yourself as My instrument.
This is right, My child. This is grace.
I need to have you so constantly aware
   that what I do is My work, My call, to My glory,
     and you are—breathe easy, My child
   but one small part of a mammoth movement of My grace
     on the earth.

44

A very important part, but a small part.
I desire only that you be pure before Me
　　that the motives of your heart be My own
　　and not based on your limited vision.
Relax as you see what I am doing with you.
　　I am honing you as My instrument.
　　I am sharpening your attentiveness to My heart and to My
　　　glory.
In this process, I am making you much more Mine
　　and, thereby, much more valuable as My instrument.

Be for Me a vessel of election.
Speak what I give you to speak
　　with no thought of who will hear and who will not hear.
It is not yours to judge
　　but yours to obey
　　　　to speak the word that I give you
　　　　to share the vision that I show you.
　　　　　I will give to that word and that vision
　　　　　the power to bring about what it says
　　　　　in the minds and the hearts of My people.

It is not you who call yourself to this work.
　　　　　It is I, the Lord, your God.
　　　　　It is I, your Beloved Father.
　　　　　It is I, the Holy Spirit, who call you.
　　　　　It will be My work.
　　It will be for My people and it will be for My glory.
I will use you as you come before Me
　　　　in the spirit of humility
　　　　in the spirit of littleness
　　　　in the spirit of renouncing your own spirit
　　　　　　　　　your own will
　　　　　　　　　your own desires
　　　　　　　　　your own vision
　　　　　　　　　your own everything.

Unite yourself to Me
        your Beloved Father
        your Beloved Bridegroom
        your Beloved Holy Spirit
and I will use you mightily.

Ark of the Covenant is My name for you.
But you would be nothing
        but an ornate
            corruptible
            wooden box
were it not for the glory
        the glory of My presence
        that you carry everywhere.
That is the point
        My dear one—

that you decrease
        so that the glory of My own face may
        shine the more brilliantly
        through you!

As Peter was called to be a fisher of people
    I am calling you too.
Come follow Me in a power that I will give you.
Leave all for Me and I will give you all.
Walk in the light and the power of the Body of which you are
    a part.
    The strength of this Body is your strength.
I have done what needs to be done.
    I have won what needs to be won.
Rest in Me. Rest in *Peter's boat.*
No evil shall touch you, for you are Mine.
No depression shall hold you, for I am your joy.
No power shall wrest you, for I am your rest.

My child,
    do not fear to go where you have never gone
    to see what you have never seen
    or to hear what no one has yet heard.
What I am doing is so new
    that it may startle you.
I give you bread of a new yeast
    wine of a new vintage.
Do not fear for the strange way I call you
    or the strange words I give you.
What is strange today will be familiar tomorrow.
What you see in part today
    will be revealed in fullness tomorrow.

I awake in you the gift of evangelism
    the gift that is like a sleeping giant
        in My church and among My people.
No other gift gives Me more joy or glory
    than your bringing your brothers and sisters
        My children, into the Kingdom.
Billions have never heard of My love for them
    or the price Jesus paid for their salvation.

That you may reach them, I share with you
    My hunger and My thirst
        My power and My authority
    that you may meet them where they are
        and bring them where I am.

If you would be of one heart, one mind, one spirit with Jesus
   yours is a call and ministry of intercession.
When you cry to Me, your Father,
   I hear not just your cry but that of My Son.
Know the power you have when you are one with Jesus
   and He is one with you.
Like Paul, count everything as so much rubbish
      that you may be one with Jesus
         and live in the mystery, the power
            and the glory of the Resurrection.[24]
Now it is a veiled mystery, but it is real.
Soon you will see it all face to face.
Then your joy will be full.

You seek a plan for intercession.
Look to Jesus for His plan:
            stand clothed in His righteousness
         agree with Jesus for the Father's perfect plan
            for those for whom you pray
         confess their sinfulness as your own
         come against all that opposes My plan
         bring down the enemy's strongholds
      in the minds of those for whom you pray
         claim their minds to be captive
      and obedient to the Lord Jesus Christ.[25]

When you were young you learned:
      God made me to know Him
            to love Him
            to serve Him in this world
         and to be happy with Him in this world
         and forever in the next.
Somehow you got that part mixed up.
      You thought you were only to know Me in the ne,
But I say to you
      that you are to know the Lord your God in the NOW.

You are to have a knowledge
a marvelous knowledge of the Lord your God
your Father in this world.
You are to *know Me*
You are to know what it is to have a Father
to have a personal Savior
to have a Holy Spirit
in this world and forever in the next.
Follow Me with the simplicity, the delight
and the joy of a child
and I will faithfully finish what I have begun.
I will lead you on from where I have brought you.
Do not hesitate to speak **My Word** boldly.
I give you holy boldness **as** I gave to Judith
to Esther and to Ruth.
I give you the anointing that was on My Son, Jesus
That you may proclaim My Kingdom by your life.
You are learning, My child, but there are times when you
forget
and like the beginning swimmer
you sink to the bottom of the pool.

My hand is always there to lift you up.
Marvel not at the times you fail
but at the times you float on, swim on
and allow My power, My love
and My Spirit to hold you up.

I equip you to drink in the mystery of Who I am
        and what I am about—
    to drink it in, but not to fully understand it.
Do not be afraid
    for you have found favor with God.
When you are weak say, "Do not be afraid
    I have found favor with my God."
I have redeemed you from your sinfulness.
You can always rise above your mistakes.
You are My precious child and I love you.
Day by day lay down your life
    that you may bring forth My life into the Kingdom.

This day the revelation of My glory
    rests upon you, My Ark of the Covenant.
You will go for Me to many lands bringing My presence.
I will not send you alone.
Someone will always stand guard for you
    and carry you as you go.
None shall harm you without suffering the penalty
    of those who raise their hand against the Most High.
Fear not to be used in this way.

My child,
You have been reading about My kings and prophets.
You have said in your heart
    "Is this the same God that calls me
        to serve and to speak with Him?"
Yes, I am the same God
    who called forth Isaiah, Jeremiah, and Daniel.
I am the same God
    who moved in the life of Ruth, Judith, and Esther.
I desire to move in your life
    to use your mouth to speak
        to call forth the moving of My Spirit.

I desire to use you
    not because you are great
        but because I
            the Lord your God, am great.
I call you, even as I called My Son
    to speak for Me
        to lay down His life for Me and for My people.
As you allow yourself to die
    like that grain of wheat falling into the ground
        I will use you.
The words that I give you will have My authority
    and will effect repentance
        healing and deliverance for My people.
My Son goes with you.
Fear not to be used by Me as
    another Jesus.
You are living in a time
    when I bring forth the body of My Son

    as a mighty power against the kingdom of Satan.
Stand in the victory of your God.

    "For Mine is the dominion,
    Mine is the power and Mine is the glory.
    Now is the salvation, the power, the kingdom,
    the authority of your God come."[26]

6

LITTLENESS

Rejoice to be like a little child and you will come
to know the bigness of your God.

We are living in the age of knowledge explosion. Some 250,000 books are published each year. Yet, all this knowledge can explode in our faces unless it helps us to know the most basic fact of our existence: God made me to know Him, to love Him, and to serve Him. Whatever else we learn from books, if they deny this, they deny everything.

We need to adopt a habit of surrender with each book we pick up. Then when we pray, "Your Move, God," He moves!

The grace of littleness is by no means a little thing
  it is a big thing to be little before your God.
It is a big grace and I gift you with it
  because in your littleness I can indeed be big.
I can be for you Yahweh, the Powerful One.
As I bless you with littleness, no matter how educated you are
  you will become like a little child.
Even your thoughts will come forth
  with a new realization of littleness.
In the past you have been heard to say
  "When I was little, I used to think."
This day I give to you the grace
      the power
      the holy wit
  to say "When I was big, I used to think."

Can you remember when you were a child? You played the game "Captain, May I." You had a captain who gave orders. You had to say, "Captain, may I?" before you followed the order.

Often as I give you an order or begin to speak to your heart, you are off to do it before you have fully heard what I have said, before you pause to check if it is really I giving you an order.

Learn to play the game with Me. When you hear an order from within, check "Father, may I?". Then do it.

Now it is My move; now it is your move! Be content to be not always on top of it, so long as I, your Father, am winning.

Be sensitive to Me and you will always be a winner.

As I anointed the lips of My prophet Isaiah with a burning
    coal[27]
    so I anoint your lips to speak with authority
        clarity, swiftness, and the simplicity of a child.

I would have you be faithful to that call
    as the prophets were faithful.
I can only use you when you are little and simple before Me.
When you get too big with ideas and plans of your own
    I cannot use you.
So let go of your need to have it all figured out.
I, your God, have it all figured out.
    I know exactly *what* I want to do.
    I know exactly *how* I want to do it.
    I know exactly *when* I want to do it.
        My time-table is perfect.
As long as you remain little,
    you will be perfectly on My timetable.

I love you, My little one,
but My anointing does not come upon you all at once.

You are somewhat like the car that is filled with gasoline
and travels a long ways.
The gasoline gets lower and lower in the tank.
So you need to stop at the filling station to get filled again.
I do this on purpose with you
that you may stay in that perfect rhythm of dependence
on Me
that you may come to Me always as your source.
It is with great purpose that you sometimes experience great
emptiness.
Sometimes you don't know if you'll make it to the next filling
station.
Sometimes you must wait.
Glorify Me for those times in which I assure you
I am faithful and I am yours.
My anointing will be there as you need it.
Be absolutely assured that when you need it—IT WILL BE
THERE.
My withholding is only so you know your absolute depen-
dence upon Me.

Be happy with the happiness of a child
content with life rather than controlling life.
Let go of complexities.
Give Me all those controversial, complicated concepts
about Who I am and what I have done.
Ask yourself: "Do these bring me to a greater knowledge
of God as my loving Father?"
Love Me with the simplicity of a child
who knows only love and trust for those who care.
Serve Me as a child serves a father
not needing to have it all together
to have it all figured out
knowing I have it all together
and all figured out from all eternity.

My child,
I have carved you on the palm of My hand.[28]
    You are Mine.
As long as you remain little
    you are Mine.
When you get too big
        too independent
        too caught up in your own things
    life becomes difficult.
Then I find it hard to use you
    and you find it difficult to be used by Me.
Rejoice to be like a little child
    and you will come to know the bigness of your God.
I hope you do not mind being called child, again and again.
Unless you become like little children
    you are not even going to get into the Kingdom of
        Heaven [29]
        much less have a high place there.

Ask Me and I will give you the grace
    to be little before the bigness of your God
      before the power of the omniscient
        omnipresent, omnipotent God.
In that littleness you can cry out to My bigness
    "Father, sovereignly move in my life
      by the power of Your Spirit.
  I am a helpless child and I need You.
Roll back the stones that keep me from walking
  in the fullness of the Resurrection.
  Lift from me that heavy spirit
  that makes me too big to be little."

My child,
I have given you My life to be your life.
This is a pure gift.
It is nothing that you have done
    nor can you claim the credit.
The most you can do is rest in My working.
I am free to be Me when you return to your littleness
    your nothingness, the grain-of-wheat-buried.
That is the key to what I can achieve in you.
Fear not, I have a plan.
*What seems dull and uneventful to you
    is high activity to Me.*
What is mystery to you
    is perfect knowledge and wisdom to Me.
As you remain little before Me
    you will begin to understand the bigness of your God.

Be holy as I am holy. [30]
Jesus has pledged Himself
    to bring you into that place of holiness.
He has laid down His life
    given His Blood
    spoken My Word that you may be holy
        as your Father is holy.

Allow your humanity to be brought into My divinity.
In this your Father is glorified.
It is entirely My doing
    your yielding, your allowing.
I ask you to do nothing that a little child cannot do.
What can a child do? It can listen
                can love
                can obey.

No matter how big the task to do
     do it with the simplicity of a child floating balloons
         or plucking flowers.
What you do for your Father is not important
     as long as you do what He wants you to do.
Accept the words and the ministry I call you to
     with the simplicity of a child
         watching all that is going on
            but not being burdened with it.

A child is not burdened with the cares of the world.
It just responds to the human scene
    with trust that its father will work it out.
If there is something to worry about
    it knows its father will do the worrying.
It is not his to be anxious
        to be troubled
        to do something about the situation
            for it has a great and mighty father
            who can handle anything.
So it simply trusts its father to make all things right.

The life of rest I have called you to
    has borne marvelous fruit that will remain.
The fruit is Mine.
Rest in your littleness
    that you might rest in My bigness.
You say to Me
    "Am I not little?
    Am I not abiding in You and You in me?"
Yes, but I will teach you a new littleness.
I will teach you what it is to be little and hidden
    as Jesus is little and hidden in the Eucharist.
I will teach you what it is to abide in Me
    as Jesus abides in Me and I in Him.[31]
In that abiding, you will come to know the power
    to say a perpetual "Yes" to the Father
    and to be perpetually little before Me.

My grace is enough for you as it was enough for Paul.
I see your weakness, My child,
    weakness in your flesh to watch with Me
        in your spirit to hear My voice
        in your will to use My gifts.

Be content to be weak
    for in it is My magnificent strength.
Those most effective in My ministry
    are those most aware of their weakness
                their inadequacy
                their imperfections
    because then they rely on My strength
                My goodness
                and My perfection.

7

LET GO

As the Spirit called Jesus into the desert to be with Me so the Spirit calls you into the desert to be with your Father.

There is no way that we can put God in second place without losing everything.

There is no way that we can give to God 99.5 percent of our lives and receive the fullness of God. The very one-half of one percent we hold back from God keeps us from receiving the totality of who God is.

It is 100 percent for 100 percent—when we say—"It's Your Move, God!"

If the Father isn't calling you
                    to do something
                    don't do it.
The answer should be "No."
When the Father is calling you to do something
          let your answer be a quick "Yes! Yes!"
Learn from Jesus to say a quick "Yes" and a quick "No"
for He is the ETERNAL YES to the Father.[32]
You need to let go of much in your life
          that is not My doing.
Needing to do your thing together with My thing
          often hinders Our thing from happening.

My child,
There is still within you
          wrestling with the memory of the past
                    the uncertainty of the future
                    the circumstances of the present.
Let go of the wrestling. Rest in Me.
What many make so complicated is so simple
          that any child can live by it.
It is total openness to the reality of the Father's love
                    to be taught
                    to be healed
                    to be set free.
That must be your life in Jesus and in Me
          a total letting go of all that contradicts.

As the Spirit called Jesus into the desert to be with Me
so the Spirit calls you into the desert to be with your
Father.
There I will show you what I am doing
and what I call you to do.
No one can come to Me except through Jesus.
You need not fear.

All you need is the heart of a child
the wonder of a child
the trust of a child.
I have been waiting long for this encounter.
Fear not to come with Jesus into the presence of your Father.

I take you, My child, into the desert
that you may know your lethargy
the lack of hunger within you
that you may strive and fight
and by violence lay hold of the **Kingdom.**[33]

I will take you more deeply into the desert than in the past
for I wish to create in you a hunger
that will make you open enough
big enough
and empty enough for Me to fill
you.
You will indeed know that it is I
and indeed you will be able to hold
the greatness of My presence
the beauty of My majesty
and the wonder of My love.
This wonder will spring from your lips
from your hands and from your ministry.
It will come with a fullness you have not known before.
I will meet you in the desert.

The ground upon which you stand is holy
    and the place to which I have called you to is holy
        for I have made it holy.
It is holy with My holiness.
I will produce holiness in you and in others.
Before the foundation of the world
    I chose you to be holy and blameless before Me.

As that palm tree bends to the wind
    so I ask that you bend in your spirit to My Spirit,
        move as I would have you move.
You wonder about all those other hopes, dreams and plans?
    What about them? You have given them to Me.
        They rest in My heart.
In My time and in My way, I will raise them up and use them.
Already I am moving among those
    for whom you have a burden and a care.
        My Spirit is moving within them.
You have given them to Me and they are Mine.
The work that I will do in them will be a sovereign work.
My power will match their needs.
How can you begin to know their needs?
    How can you begin to know My power?
        You will see.
My power can meet every need of those who come to Me.
You say to Me, "God, really?"
    I say to you, My child, really!
I plan to surprise you, and you will be surprised.
There is nothing I cannot and will not do
    for those who come to Me in trust.

The hand that created the whole world
    has you and all you love resting in it.
I hear you pray, "Let it be."
According to your faith, let there be healing, freedom,
    love, restoration, everything you need
    that you may come with your loved ones into My
    Kingdom.

It isn't so much what you have to do
　　　as what you need to cease doing
　　　　　that I may be active in you.

　　　If you could only see what I see
　　　　　you would rejoice that I
　　　　　　　have so totally prepared the way for you.
　　Rejoice in the plan that the heart of your Father
　　　　has for you from all eternity.
　　Walk with your hand in the hand of your Father.
　　If I have the whole world in My hand

　　I have also the future of all you love in My hand.
　　　Willingly
　　　　　joyfully
　　　　　　　trustingly LET GO
　　of all you have in your hand that you may know
　　　only the hand of your Father.

　　When you begin a task in your own will
　　　　　and feel within you that check
　　　know *it is I, your Father,*
　　　　　reminding you to pause
　　　　　　　to turn from what is you
　　　　　　　　and be fully turned to Me.

To be one with your Father
　　　means to be one thought with His thought
　　　　　　one word with His Word
　　　　　　one energy with His energy
　　　　　　one power with His power
　　　　　　one mind with His mind
　　　　　　one spirit with His Spirit
　　　　　　one plan with His plan.

To be one with Me
     means to lose yourself in the heart of your Father
       so that we are no longer two but just one.
My child,
    for almost two thousand years
      My Son has been praying for this oneness
        that you may be one in Me
         as Jesus is one in Me.[34]
I promise you, we will be one.

Look not for confirmation that you are on the right path.
    I will provide assurances when you least expect them.
I am pleased with your trust of Me.
I have all things in control.
I have power to change every circumstance.
It pleases Me when your eyes are upon Me
    and not on the circumstances.
It pleases Me when you call upon the power of the Word
                the Blood
                the name of
                Jesus.

You are learning to walk in the authority
    and power of your Beloved.
Do not lose heart, for I give you My heart.

What determines what you would do for Me, your Father?
      Is it money?
      Is it time?
      Is it energy?
      Is it what other people will think?
      Is there anything you would not do
        for lack of these?

Yield your weakness to My strength
    your fears to My love
    your whole being to My eternal plan.
I can only use a yielded vessel for My purposes.
When you forget who I am and who you are
        you experience defeat
             fear
               confusion.
Why fret and worry as though you did not have a Father?
Why rely on your own resources
    when Mine are at your disposal?

My child, it is not only right but imperative
    that you let go of everything and everyone
        that keeps Me from being your Father.
I am ready with infinite love and eternal wisdom
    to supply all your needs.
I am ready to quell all that is restless
    to bring light to all that is darkness
    to silence what is noisy within you.
There is something within you
    that cries out to be somebody and to do something.
I will take this from you.
Jesus allowed Himself to take on a death of degradation
    to earn for you the grace of totally letting go
        so that My Kingdom may come.
I delight to see that you do not fear this fire
    but that you desire it with all your heart.

Cease striving!
As you cease, My activity will begin.
Lay down your busyness in My hand.
I will pick it up and do all that needs to be done.
Hunger and thirst for more of My Spirit.
I can only fill what is empty.
I can only be what you allow Me to be
and do what you allow Me to do
as you die to all that is not Me.
There is living only as there is dying
Resurrection as there is death
Pentecost as there is an Upper Room of waiting and praying.

Remember
"Easy does it."
When things become difficult
when you are doing your thing
Stop! Step Back! Check!
Is this yours or Mine?
When it is your God working, easy does it.
Let God be God and you be you!

Rest tonight in the power and pervading beauty of My love.
Before you get into bed
    lay at My feet all the graces
        all the blessings
        all the goodness of this day.
Offer all of it again to Me in worship
    and let go of it
        finished or unfinished
        full or unfull.
Allow Me to have complete reign.
Tomorrow will have new gifts
            new surprises
            new openings of glory.

71

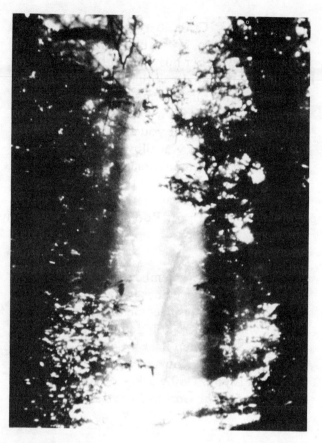

Rest in complete adoration of Me this night.
Let go of where you are
     of what you are doing
     of what you understand
         and what you do not understand
     of where you have been
         and of where you will be going.
Allow Me to be a Father who takes you by the hand
    and leads you on a path you do not know.
I lead you.
So let go of it all before Me tonight
    and let your resting body speak this night of adoration.
I am with you.

8

WORSHIP AND REST

How important it is for you to come before Me,
your Father, in the stillness of My heart, that I
might allow you to know what it is to be still in
the presence of your Father.

*Invite God to look deep into your eyes for what is there,
what He has put and planted there, what He is doing there.*
*Look into the eyes of God; allow yourself to love God
with your eyes. Rest in that gaze! Rejoice in that contemplation! Surrender as you pray, "It is* Your Move, God!"

I am as near to you as your next thought.
When you have surrendered your whole thought world to Me
    I take over and I put My thoughts into your mind.
Then your thoughts and words are Mine
    and Mine are yours.
This oneness is My work.
Rest in it. Worship in it.
Worship is your life poured out
    your will to follow My will
    your thoughts to become My thoughts
    Your whole being in a service of praise.
I am pleased, My child,
    with the worship that is taking place within you
        moment by moment and task by task.
Sometimes in worship I call you to repent
    that I may purify in you all that has not been
        worship and praise of your God.

This is no new call I put upon your life
It has been there for a long time.
Often I have called you in the night
    and in the early morning hours.
But you have rationalized that call
    and excused yourself because of fatigue.
I have had pity on that.
In repentance is your strength.[35]
Ponder today *Who you deny*
        When you deny your God.

You have passed into new life with your God.
You have entered into Me
and I have entered into you in a new way.
Now that you have come to this holy place
you wonder *What do I do here?*
Rest here. Rest in My love.
Rest in My activity.

Your activity is finished.
Let yourself be tuned in
 to see what it is We are doing
 to listen to what We are saying
 to be in worship of what is happening
 to live your life together with Jesus' life
 constantly immolated for the glory of the Father.
Whatever does not fit
with that life of pure worship
does not fit.
Let go of it.
Come back to the state of worship.
As you come back again and again
your life will flow
in a state of perpetual worship of the Father.

I, your almighty Father
 have pledged Myself
  to be with you
  to be the Word upon your lips
  the Initiator of your actions.

I have been your teacher
	and I will teach through you.
I have been your Healer
	and I will heal through you.
I would not leave you to yourself
	anymore than I would have left Jesus to Himself.
As He did nothing on His own
	so you need do nothing on your own.
I am with you.

Your old life is gone
	like that trail of smoke that comes when you blow out a
	candle.
		It evaporates.
		It is no more.
So your old life is no more, it's gone.
		It's dead.
	Only that *New Life* remains.
Look to that new life as the source of what you think
						what you say
						what you are to do.
What is happening within you is so total
		so complete
				that there is no describing this purification
					of your senses
						of your inner being.
You are being transformed by the living God.
You dare not comprehend it.
You need only to say a continued
				Yes! Let it be! Be it done!

How important it is for you to come before Me, your Father,
in the stillness of your heart
to rest in the stillness of My heart
that I might speak to you
that I might allow you to know what it is to be still
in the presence of your Father
to know no anxious thought or desire
to know nothing except the stillness
the quiet
the rest
the content of a child
in the presence of its Father.
If you would only do this
you would indeed know that I am God.
You would know it in your mind
for I would open your mind to see that I am God.
You would know it in your heart
for I would open your heart to experience that I am God.
You would know it in your spirit
for through My Spirit I would reveal that I am God.

I hear you pray
"Speak, Lord, for your servant is listening."[36]
But I say
"Speak child, your God is listening!"
Not only am I listening
but I am effecting that which I hear you pray.
Did I not promise
Ask and it shall be given to you!
Knock and it will be opened to you![37]
My delight is in your asking, your seeking, your knocking
for then I am able to pour forth
from that bountiful storehouse of graces
whatever is your need.

Let worship be your supreme occupation.
Come back to Me again and again
    with your gratitude and your praise.
        Keep your eyes on Me.
That means off of you and on your loving Father.
When you are totally surrendered to My purpose
           I am working.
        Rest means to rest.
        Cease activity means to cease.
        Release your need to understand.
Know that from all eternity I know what I plan to do.
        Is there anything impossible for Me?
          My child,
I am pouring into your life My life.
    You dare not choose to fully comprehend.
Learn to rest like a child—a very small child—
    trusting in a Father's love and care.
        I couldn't love you more than I do.
I couldn't care more for what is happening within you.

I am doing a delicate work within you.
        It takes a delicate hand!
        It takes a Father's time!
    I don't ask you to do these things.
You don't have to do anything that a child cannot do.
        Rest! Listen! Love!
But you have been doing more than that.
    You have been reaching out.
    You have been grabbing hold of things.
    You have been restless with your listening.
As you seek Me for forgiveness, I readily forgive you
    for I remember that you are but clay.
I continue to hold you in the palm of My Hand.
    I continue to form you in the palm of My Hand.
I am forming you to do a small part of a mighty work.

My word to you is steady.
    Keep a steady eye upon Me.
        Look to Me above every person.
Keep a steady ear for My word.
        Listen to Me above every sound around you.
        Listen for I am speaking.
I am closer to you than the breath you breathe
    the thoughts you think, the words you say.
Have I not given to you My heart with all its feelings, attitudes, desires?
Have I not given to you all that I am, for all that you are?
Where in the world could you have struck a better exchange?

Do not fear! Do not worry!
A princess does not look good with worry lines upon her face.
What I have ordained I will accomplish.
What I have planned I will do.
    You are professing faith in a sovereign God.
    It is sovereignly that I choose to work.
Your call was given by Me for that is the way I plan to work
    in you, and in My Church.

Don't expect to understand.
    Don't expect it to make sense.
    Divine sense. Yes!
Simply ask and I will give you abundant wisdom.
I lift all worry from you.
You are responsible to listen, to follow, to trust.
    I appreciate when you ask.
    I could do everything without you, but I choose to use
        you.

There is a great wave of power that goes forth
        great waves of power that you do not see
        because you are too small to see.
I would have you see these waves of power as you gaze into
    My Heart.
      My love for you is sufficient cause for rejoicing
        without seeing the results.
I am setting you on the crest of the wave
    that you may ride with Me
        and I want you to enjoy it!

My child, when you feel most alone
you can be most with Me.
Think of what it means to be *with* your Creator
    who made the universe
    who called you out of nothingness
    who loves you with an everlasting love
    who knows your comings and your goings
    your risings and your fallings.

No matter how things seem to be falling apart
know they are together when we are together.
No power in heaven or on earth
can separate you from your Father
except your choice to be separated from Me.
Even when you make that choice
in a moment of fear, doubt or weakness
know that I await you to make the choice
to return to Me.
Then we will be together again.
You in Me and I in you.
As Jesus is one with Me and I am one with Jesus
so We desire to be one with you.
This Oneness is not something for the future.
It is for today.

Never fear, when the time is over
it will all be there
in your mind and in your spirit.
All you need to know, you will know.
All you need to become, you will have become.
Allow yourself to absorb the depth, the height,
the length, and the breadth of your Father's love
and it will infallibly happen.

Hands off means hands off
so I can get My hands on.
Know that I am God, not you!
Listen to Me, My child.
Out of listening will come light
Out of light will come direction and strength.
As you enter into My rest
you will enter into My eternal activity.
You are to fast not only from food
but from doing and needing to fully understand.
To be where you are powerfully used
is not where it's at
but to be where you are totally surrendered.

Yes, My child,
it has been a silent day.
You have wondered—Where is my Father?
Where is my Daddy?
My PaPa?
Why isn't He talking to me?
Why am I so alone?
I have been with you
present in the silence
forming you in the palm of My hand.
Rest there.
Be content with nothingness.
Be content with nothing going on
except Me.
I am going on!

I have brought you a long, long way.
There have been moments when you wondered whether you'd
make it.
You have made it!
You have arrived at a place of rest
that I have prepared for you.
Now all I ask is that you truly rest
that you cease striving.
My rest is your rest.
Not only enter, but remain there.
I will do it all.
Hush!
Shhhhh!

9

BATTLE

I am a God of Light. I call you to shed the works of darkness and stand in My Light.

This is the day, the hour, the decade for us to look to God, our Father, to do for us, His children, the impossible: to fulfill the impossible dream, to beat the unbeatable foe, to move with His power against all powers that would destroy us from within and from without.

When "Washington for Jesus" was being planned, one of the Senators said that it had been expressed and believed by many that barring a miracle they would give our country five years to be destroyed by financial ruin, military conquest, or moral corruption. Our country is the great helpless giant that can only be rescued by the sleeping giant that is the Church— that is, God's people getting it together.

The same Holy Spirit that brooded in the Book of Genesis over the watery chaos is brooding today over the chaotic mess that people have made of creation. God is waiting for a whole-souled cry from His children,—"Come Holy Spirit renew the face of the earth—it is Your Move, God."

This is divine warfare you are in
    and it requires divinity to fight it.
You cannot fight it with your natural mind.
    You cannot fight it with your natural spirit.
It must be fought in the Spirit
    and so I will teach you to fight in the Spirit.
I will teach you to bring down those forces
    by the power of My Blood
        and by the sword of My Word.

I will teach you, My child,
      to take every thought captive in obedience to Me as you
          pray:
              In the name of Jesus
             by the power of His Blood
             in the authority of His Word
    I come against idle speculations and every lofty thing
        that lifts itself up against the knowledge of God.[38]
    I bring down the powers of darkness that rule the mind
        and the feelings of My loved ones.
      I loose them from the judgment of others
and I claim them to be totally reconciled to God their Father
        and their Lord Jesus Christ.

Are you weary, shaken and chastened?
You shall be strengthened
    by the power of My Spirit
    in your inner person.
You shall be rooted and grounded
in the knowledge of your Lord Jesus Christ
and filled with the fullness of your God.
    For am I not able to do exceedingly
    abundantly beyond all that you ask or desire?[39]
You have been before Me
in perseverance and prayer.

You have prayed the Word
      pondered the Word
      claimed the Word
      and stood on the Word.
Now I, your God, will stand on My Word
and bring My Word made flesh into your flesh.

There is no time when you will ever come so far
    that you will not need My Word.
My Word will eternally separate the marrow from the bone. [40]
    It will separate all that is not Me from all that is Me.
In your waking and in your sleeping
    you need the power of My Word.
You need to rest in the power of My Word
    for there is infinite delight
                    joy
                    strength
                    and direction in the power of My
                    Word.
As it was necessary for Jesus in His humanity
        to do battle using the force of My Word,
    so it will be necessary for you to do battle
        by the force of that Word—
        IT IS WRITTEN
    Heaven and earth will pass away,
    but My Word shall never pass away. [41]

If I your Father have the whole world in My Hand
    then surely I can hold the whole world of you.
I can transform the whole of you.
    I can make you holy.
I can use you without all the things you think you need
    that you are still striving for.
I can best teach you when you are truly humble before Me.
The enemy is best thwarted
    when you are poured out in adoration before Me.

I have the master plan
        and I demand absolute obedience.
            Obedient love.
    Delayed obedience is disobedience.
    You cannot afford to delay your obedience.

88

When I speak, I expect you to obey
        with the simplicity of a child
        with the quickness of a child
        with the delight of a child
    who loves and trusts his father
    and knows the consequences for disobedience
    or delayed obedience.

My child,
It is not just that I have taken over your mind
        and your spirit to do a work for Me
            but I have taken over your anxieties
                            your cares
                            your fears
                            your worries
                            your inadequacies
        that I may do a work for you!
Do not take them back.
They are Mine
    as you are Mine!
            As you trust in My power
                you will not be lacking power
                        for anything I call you to do.
            Stand in My power
                and you will stand in My victory.
            You will not be part of a weak, cowardly army.
            Together with your brothers and sisters
                        together with Me
                your strength will be invincible
                your power will be unconquerable.

You will *beat the unbeatable foe.*
You will know the *impossible dream* is for you.
It is the reality of your life lived in Me
        and My life lived in you.

I gift you this day with an inner vision
    so you will look neither to the right nor to the left.
The spirit within you shall clearly say
    This is the way; walk in it. [42]
As you walk, you shall not only walk
    but you shall leap
      you shall skip
      you shall jump
      and you shall run in the way
        I call you to run.
I call you to join Me in a dance of victory.
As the Father will dance [43]
    so you too will dance in the day of joy
      for the victory that is Mine
        for My church and for My people.
There shall be rejoicing in the heavens
    and there shall be rejoicing on the earth.
There shall be rejoicing in the hearts
    and in the minds of all men
      for what I am doing.

I gift you with power to be singleminded before Me with My
    mind.
It is true that My thoughts are above your thoughts
    like the heavens are above the earth
    but more and more you will discover
      that My thoughts are indeed your thoughts.
I am as close to you as your next thought.

Yield your mind to My mind, and I will gift you
    with discernment to quickly see the thoughts
        that come from the Holy Spirit
            your human spirit
            or the evil spirit.
I will give you the power to switch from what is useless or evil
    as easily as you switch TV channels.
My child, you question if I can really speak to you
    with such power
        such directness
        such control.
Ask yourself if someone sells his mind out to a demonic
    power
    does the enemy not fully take over?
Could I do less for My children?

I will use you as a powerful warrior
    to bring many people into the Kingdom.
Your words as you teach
    your praying and My people resting in My Spirit
        will do a work of fighting.
Sometimes I call you to fight in one way.
    Other times I call you to fight in another.
But always the call will be the call of My Spirit.
You are to be tuned in to My Spirit
    so where I am, you may be
        and where you are, I assure you, We will be.

I will not have a fearful people
    but I will have a faith-filled people.
I will have a fearless people
    radiant with faith in their Father's love.
You will go forth like mighty giants filled with My Spirit.
As the saints went forth with courageous faith
    you will go and you will do
        a mighty work
    that will bring to the minds of unbelievers
        the realization that your God lives.

Jesus was like you in all things save sin
    that you might be graced to know how to live
      and how to handle the enemy.
It is in closeness to your Father
    that you will be able to discern the enemy
      with each fresh scheme of his.
There are places and times
    that you need to be careful.
Know your vulnerable spot
    and yield it to Me.

      I am a God of light.
      I call you to shed the works of darkness
        and to stand in My light.
      Let go of all the darkness rooted in your past
        that comes to you from other generations.
      There are works of darkness
        that go back hundreds of years.
      I give you authority to say:
          "Darkness, you are to leave!
          I am a child of the Light.
          All darkness in my roots must go."
    Can I not work miracles as I worked of old?
    Can I not roll back sickness and disease
      and the things that destroy you
      as I rolled back the waters of the Red Sea?
    Can I not hold them back
      roll them back
      so they have no more hold on you?

      As the darkness grows around you
        My light grows within you.
      As My light grows
        the darkness will not affect you.
      My child, you must discern the battle.

You cannot walk with one foot in each kingdom.
You cannot walk with one part of you in darkness
 and the other part in light.
If you are to be a child of light
 you must walk wholly in light. [44]
Repent of everything that is work of darkness.
Darkness cannot exist in My light.
As you cast it out
 you enter into the center of the battle around you
 the battle against the kingdom of darkness.
I give you My eyes to see
 and My ears to hear.
I give you My mind to discern
 that you may walk totally in Me
 as a child of light.
This is a new season.
There is no turning back.
There is only going forward with your eyes upon Me
 your mind and heart set like flint
 to go like Jesus to the cross.
The glory of the Lord shall rest upon you
and your city.
Have I not given My angels charge over you? [45]
And shall I not send forth in this time of darkness
a force of My angelic hosts to guard you
 to fight for you
 to be for you a mighty force
 against the powers of darkness?

Even as Satan
has unleashed his forces upon the face of the earth
so I have sent forth myriads of angels
    to stand guard over My people
    to be for your protection
    to bring about victory in your minds
                  in your homes
                  in your families
                  in your cities
                  in your churches.

Some will feel the effects of angels.
Others will experience angels doing battle for them.
Michael and his warriors come to do battle for all.
Be for Me
a people believing in the help that I give.
It will not be victory in your strength.
        It will be victory in My strength.
        It will be victory in My power.
      It will be victory according to My mind
          and according to My Spirit.
Not by might nor by power
but by My Spirit, says the Lord.[46]
You shall stand in victory this day.

The mind is often where the battle is fought.
   It is Satan's target of attack.
If he can enter with his negative forces of
   unbelief
         cynicism
               resentment
                  rebellion
                     confusion
then he has ground to wage his battle.
My child,
      do not be intimidated
            by the seeming strength of the enemy.
Though he goes about like a roaring lion [47]
      he is no lion.
My Son is the Lion of Judah.
The power of Satan compared to Mine
      is like that of a cockroach!

10

FIRE AND JUDGMENT

Are there things within you that need to be consumed by the fire of My Spirit? Do not fear that fire.

Several years ago a priest from India shared this observation: I see two things holding back the move of the Holy Spirit across the face of the earth. First, a superficial knowledge of what it is, and second, we are scared to death what might happen if we allowed God to touch our life with His power.

If these are holding back the Spirit across the face of the earth then perhaps these are the very things that are holding back the Spirit in our lives.

There is no excuse anymore for having a superficial knowledge of what God is doing or ready to do. We need to read the signs of the times to see what He is doing and move with what He is showing us.

As for the fear, it can be cast out with an infilling of love. Neither ignorance nor fear will serve as valid excuses when we soon stand before the Lord of lords, the King of kings and the Judge of all men.

My child,
I call you to a season of fasting
     turning away from the desires of the flesh
     turning more completely
        to the desires of your God.
Turn to Me
     and I will turn to you.
I will open your ears that you may hear Me
     your eyes that you may see Me.
I will do a work of cleansing, burning
     and refining within you
        as you fast and pray. [48]

There is much that needs to be cleansed
      much that needs to come under My judgment.
I ask you not to fear this
for I, your Father
will sovereignly work in your mind
in your spirit and in your body
when you come before Me fasting.
As Jesus fasted and prayed
     before His time of ministry
     now you are being called into the desert
     to fast and to pray.
Join your fast with the power of His fast.
I will pour forth upon you
that same anointing that I poured upon Jesus
as He began His public ministry.
That anointing will bring victory
     where you would have known defeat
     light where you would have been in darkness
     knowledge where you would not have known
     what to do.
My child,
I am pleased this day with your fast
     and your faithfulness.

You have wondered:
     "What is going on here?"
     "Is anything going on here?"

I say to you:
     The sovereign moving of the living God
     is going on in the depths of your being
          in your heart
          in your mind
          in your spirit.
     Your God is cleansing
          healing
          restoring.

Rest in the knowledge that I am at work.
Say "Yes!" to the mind-blowing way I am working.
Just as cities and homes are built in a day
        with the transforming work of modern machines
        so hearts and lives are being transformed
        by the work of My Spirit.

**You are living in a time
when there is not much time
so the work to be done
needs to be done quickly.**

The foundation I am building within you
will endure storms and persecutions
the hard times as well as the beautiful times.
I am building a foundation of trust
        surrender
                and abiding love of your Father.

YOU CAN TRUST YOUR GOD!
Trust Me as Jesus trusted Me.
I am worthy!

My child,
You wonder if you are ready.
Are you ready for the Bridegroom
        to come for you as the Bride?
Individually, as a church, as a people,
        is your lamp ready—is it trimmed?
Are there things within you that need to be consumed
        by the fire of My Spirit,
        done away with by the judgment of My Spirit?
I have spoken to you through your leaders.
        What I have not been able to achieve
        through the outpouring of gifts and power
        I will achieve in a baptism of fire and judgment.

Do not fear that fire.
Submit to it with the trust of a child
    who knows its father will bring no harm.
As Isaac trusted Abraham [49]
    you must trust Me
        so like gold you may be purified.
Your love for Me will be brought to perfection
    when you can face the day of judgment without fear.

Ask Me, My child,
    and I will show you areas in your life
    that have not been led by My Spirit
        thoughts
            words
                things you have done or left undone.
        When I bring to your mind
        an area of sin or weakness
        submit that failure to My judgment
        and all similar moments of sin
            from your whole life.
        Be willing to admit your sinfulness.
        It is not your sinfulness that bothers Me.
        But what you do to cover it up.

Open yourself to the cleansing fire of My Spirit
    and I will burn up all that is rubbish.
Do not fear
to have Me enter your life in this way.
I am a merciful judge now, and
I will have pity on you.
I am merciful!
        I will forgive all your debts
            though they be in the millions.

Within you I have placed the dual desire to face your God
    and to be effaced in His presence.
Sometimes, indeed, you have faced Me
    and sometimes you have been effaced in My presence.
It is not the good in you that is effaced
    but that which is the work of darkness
                        weakness
                    and sinfulness.

    You too, My child,
    must have mercy upon your brothers and sisters.
        You must forgive others
        if you are to be forgiven!
    If I am to be a merciful Judge in your life
        you must reach out in forgiveness
            to all who have hurt you.
    Ask!
    I will give you the help you need to forgive others
        just as I forgive you.

I speak to you a heavy word
but I want you to receive it with a light heart.
        Never before have My children lived
            in such serious decision-making times.
        Never before has the force and power of destruction
                threatened so many.
        Never before has the power of the Father's love
            been so ready to move in your life.
The decision you face is not how to handle the darkness
        but how to open yourself to the light;
not how to handle the hate and destruction that threatens
        but how to open yourself to love;
not how to create new sources of power in this
                energy crisis
        but how to discover the dynamo of energy within you
            that is your God!

Like so many grains of wheat
    I have gathered you from the fields.
With My own hands, I have crushed
                        broken
                              and ground
      that wheat into a fine meal.
I will continue to knead you
    and make you into bread to be broken
        and fed to the multitudes.
For you are My Body
    and you are My Blood
        given for the salvation of the world.

    Sometimes you sound like Peter.
        You even act like Peter.
            I need to send you roosters to crow!
If you are to grow under the fire of My Spirit
      you must submit to My judgment
          and be brought to a flow of conviction
      and repentance.

    Whatever resists the Father's love
        is an obstacle to the flow of grace.
My Spirit reminds you to remain the
      grain-of-wheat-fallen-to-the-ground-dead
      that I may live in you.
To get too big or to live independent of Me
    is mischief and must be put down!
You must return to your
      grain-of-wheat-buried state.
Then the Holy Spirit is free!
    Jesus is free!
        The Father is free!
           And you are free!

My beloved child,
Silence your words
    that My Word may come forth.
There will be times
    when I stop you in the middle of a sentence
        or in the middle of a task.
Be sensitive to the whispering of My Spirit
    and realize where you have not been holy.
He will show you
    where your thoughts have not been holy
    and your words stem from selfish ambition.
He will show you
    how often the things you do or leave undone
    have their origin in your human spirit
        or an evil spirit
    rather than in My Holy Spirit.
Submit these to the fire of My Spirit that you may be
    purified
          transformed
             made holy.

My child, I rejoiced with you
    as you celebrated reconciliation with Me.
You have been purified, cleansed, and made whole.
If you could only see what is happening
    what joy would be yours!
You see only the surface.
    I see the reality.
Rejoice in the song of Mary:
      My soul magnifies the Lord
    And my spirit rejoices in God,
      My personal Saviour,
        For He who is mighty
    Has done great things for me
      And Holy is His name! [50]

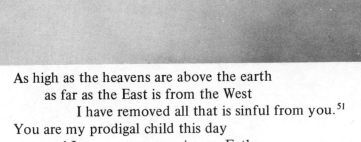

As high as the heavens are above the earth
as far as the East is from the West
I have removed all that is sinful from you.[51]
You are my prodigal child this day
and I am your magnanimous Father.

11

REPENTANCE, HEALING, SALVATION

This day you will become a new creation. All that is old has passed away.

King David prayed, "I give thee thanks for I am fearfully, wonderfully made" (Ps. 139).

Little did he know then what we know now of the wonder in each of us, of 60,000 billion living cells each with the DNA blueprint for our entire body, of the 10 million brain cells as complicated as the most complicated computer, of the 2,000 gallons of blood being pumped through 60,000 miles of blood vessels daily by a heart the size of a fist.

Without considering inflation, it would cost man more than six million dollars to construct even the bionic man. Yet He who created us can recreate any part of our mind, body, or spirit FREELY out of love. We are fearfully, wonderfully made by a Creator who is Father,

Loving Father,
Omnipotent Creator,
King of kings and
Lord of lords.

He speaks to us as a most loving Father. He awaits our prayer of surrender.

It's Your Move, God!

Each new day brings a new challenge for you
   to be
      yet
         more
            open
      yet
         more
            filled
      yet
         more
            emptied.

I can only fill a vessel that is emptied.
I can only reshape what is resting on My potter's wheel[52]
    content with its brokenness
      desiring to be made whole.
Leave yourself in My creative Hands
    and you will know a new wholeness
      that comes from a new brokenness.
You must first accept the beauty of brokenness
    if you are to know the joy of wholeness.

If you thought that was funny to you
    you should have seen Me laughing.
When you come before Me in repentance
    admitting the things that separate you
      one from another and from Me.
I come in with My giant vacuum sweeper, the Holy Spirit,
    who "wufts" them right up into the heart of your God.
I encourage you even now
    to laugh at the incongruities in life.
I gift you with a godly sense of humor and holy laughter.

The more you are content to be a part of humanity
    the more you will be able to partake of My divinity.
It is not the divinity of Jesus
    that My children have trouble accepting
    it is His humanity.
Therefore they have a problem accepting their own humanity.
I am a God of the everyday
A God who delights to sit at your breakfast table
to walk with you in the market place.
Allow Me to be not just Lord of your life
*   but to be part of every part of your life.*

Allow Me to be your Vinedresser
    and I will show you what is unproductive in your life.
    "That's the way I am," you often say.
    But I can change that.
    I am not that way!
I am the Divine Pruner.[53]
    As you allow Me, I will cut away
        all that is not My planting.
I will reveal all that needs healing.
    I will show you ways you have been hurt.
I will listen when you cry:

> *"Father, I want to forgive with Your forgiveness*
> *those who have done me wrong*
> *those who have taken advantage of me*
> *those who have hurt or damaged me in any way*
> *and kept me from becoming what I desired to*
> *become*
> *and even kept me from Your love.*

> *"Father, I even forgive You.*
> *Forgive me for that.*
> *Forgive me for the things I thought You did against*
> *me*
> *for the times I thought You were against*
> *me*
> *because of what You allowed and what You*
> *didn't.*

> *"I forgive myself for the times I wouldn't allow myself*
> *to be a child of the Father*
> *for the times I allowed myself to be*
> *destroyed*
> *by sin and works of darkness.*

> *"I forgive what I have done to others.*

> *"Father, I forgive and now I know that You forgive me."*

Intercede for your brothers and your sisters
    who are not faithful.
I do not call you to be their judge.
    I call you to be their intercessor
        to stand with Jesus interceding for them.
Yours is a ministry of intercession and reconciliation.
As you plead with Me
    I will bring about conviction
                conversion
                and desire to return to Me.
I will forgive them
    even as I have forgiven you.
Cry out for the most hopeless
    for the most godless.
If the good thief on the cross could turn to My Son and say
    "Remember me when you come into your Kingdom,"[54]
        they, too, can turn.
This day the most despicable
    the most impossible
        the most unbelievable can be with Me in Paradise.
For you have stood with Jesus in the gap.[55]
You have pleaded for your brother and your sister.
    There is no more important work
        on the face of the earth
    than the work of intercession
        for that is the work
    that I have given to Jesus.

He spent thirty years in hidden life
    three years in public life,
        and almost two thousand years making intercession
for you!

There are countless souls who live without hope
    who think they are going to hell because of their past
    because of the confusion in which they were raised
    because of the confusion in which they've lived
    because they turned from Me in their youth
        and now live without hope.
Tell them: **There is hope.**
        Hope if they turn to Me
        if they say to Me
        "Father, be to me a father."
Like the Prodigal Son, they can return to Me[56]
    for I have been longing for them.

My love has been searching them out.
    I have been speaking to them in the night and in the day
        but many have not heard My voice.
            They are locked in their sins.
But they are not locked so permanently
    that they cannot be set loose.
They must simply turn to Me, their loving Father.
I will reveal Jesus as their personal Saviour.

My Son paid the price
    so no matter what their life has been
    or what their sinful condition might be
    no matter how they turned from Me
    if they will say: "God, come into my life,"
I will come in!

If they will turn to Jesus and say:
        "Jesus, be my personal Saviour.
        Forgive me. I'm sorry.
        Cover my sins with Your Blood.
        Come into my heart and my life.
        Thank you for coming into my heart and my life."

This day they will become a new creation.[57]
    All that is old has passed away.
    All that is work of darkness
                bitterness
                hate
                sin
                fear
                depression
    all that has been hopelessness over the years
    all the times they have said
        "I am going to hell"
    all these are past for now they can say:
"I am going to Heaven!"

12

FATHER'S LOVE

Come to Me as your Father and I will teach you
to experience My presence. There is no energy
crisis in your God.

The realization of the Father's love was the greatest thrust in the life of Jesus. Jesus needed to GROW IN AN EXPERIENCE OF HIS FATHER'S LOVE. That is the simplest, the most profound, the most complicated task we are called to—a growing realization that the Father loves us; that He loves ME!

Our greatest mission to our families, friends, and the world is bringing them to realize that the Father loves THEM! *In this, they will experience salvation, healing, deliverance, and a new fullness of the knowledge and love of God.*

This will be ours as we pray—"It's Your Move, God!"

You have within you, My child,
　　a dual desire to face God and to be effaced
　　　　in His presence.
Bring Me that desire.
　　I will give you glimpses of what it means
　　　　to face your Father.
Just glimpses, for no one can fully see My face and live.
I will give you glimpses that you may experience
　　　　the presence of Eternal Light
　　　　the presence of Eternal Glory
　　　　the arms of Everlasting Love.
In this light you will see Light.
　　In this glory you will know Glory.
　　　　In this love you will be consumed by Eternal Love.
There is much I desire to show you even in a veiled way.
As your growing knowledge is
　　your growing love and service will be.

Beloved,
    Abide in My love. [58]
This is both a Divine invitation and command.
    Abide means to live.
To live on in My love is to turn your back
        on all that contradicts My Love.
You cannot abide in My Love
        and abide in the spirit of the world.
Use the things of the world
        but do not let them use you.
Do not let them control you
            or become idols in your life.
Nothing should be of real concern to you
        except your right relationship with Me
            and your right attitude toward others.

This day you have entered with Jesus
        into a new and holy place.
Do not hesitate to enter and remain.
    I am here to be for you a Father
                to be for you the Alpha and the Omega [59]
            the beginning and the end
            and all the in-betweens.
To be all the in-betweens means that in each moment
    each thought, each feeling of panic you have
        I am here to be your *all in all.*

My child,
I delight in your wordless words
        for what I have done in your heart.
I give you not just the fruit of your time
            on the mountaintop
        but the fruit of the thirty years Jesus spent
            in hidden life.

Rejoice in that sharing of His life with your life.
Only as Jesus came to know My love in those hidden years
        was He empowered to know My love in His active years.
As Jesus was called to spend more time in His hidden life
            than in His active life
        you are called to more time in your hidden life
            to grow in your Father's love.

My child,
You come to Me desiring to see My face.
You shall find Me in the faces
        of those I call you to serve.
More and more you will recognize My face in the crowds
        and My face when you are alone.
I desire to reveal to you
        the face of your Father
            the face of your Beloved Jesus
                the face of the Holy Spirit.

        Your Father is ready to speak to you.
        It has nothing to do with your being ready
                nothing to do with your being worthy.
        I am worthy and ready.
        You, too, are ready if you rest in Me.

Come to Me as your Father
        and I will teach you to experience My presence.
There is no energy crisis in your God.
The crisis is in you
        in your failure to believe and understand
                that My infinite power can totally match your need.

I want you to know the fullness of My love
    for each member of your family.
I am first of all, their Father.
    They are My creation.
I will renew and restore them as I promised.
    Listen to how I will do it.
I don't ask *you* to do the impossible but *I* will!
I will roll back stones of resistance
    of fear, of indifference
        as you look to Me.
See this miracle in your faith-imagination as you pray.
See My Spirit bringing new life
    to all who have been devastated
        through sin, suffering, and circumstance.

There is much I desire to teach you
    about the great mystery of Love.
All eternity is not long enough to stand, to kneel
    to lie prostrate before such Love.
        "THIS IS MY BODY" [60]
means yours, too; you are one with Jesus.
When you are totally surrendered to My Life, it is finished.
        The rest is up to Me.

Do not love the world nor the things of the world
    for if anyone loves the world
    the love of the Father is not in him.
All that is in the world
    the lust of the eyes
        and the boastful pride of life
is not from the Father. [61]
You cannot be a half-and-half person with half of the things
    of the world and half of the things of your Father.
You must make a choice.

Soon all those things you have clung to and
chosen to love in place of your Father;
all those things you have worked, slaved
and given your life for
will have passed like a ship in the night.
But those who choose Me
will live in My love forever.

Allow Jesus to teach you the love of the Father
and how to grow in holiness.
He will teach you what it is like
to be truly poor in spirit
and full of love for all peoples.
As Jesus grew in wisdom, age and grace
He grew in the knowledge of My love
as it is spoken in the Word.
He grew in knowledge of My infinite desire
that you be saved, healed and set free.
Learn from Jesus the depths of My love
and My yearning
to make you holy as I am holy.[62]

I AM TOTAL LOVE.
For all eternity, My name has been Love.
It is My nature to love.
I cannot *not* love that which I have created.
But YOU can turn from My love.
You can refuse it.
When you who have refused My love
repent
I will still be here and be for you
all I said I would be.
When you are open to Me, I am open to you.
When you turn back to Me, I am already turned to you.
I have never turned from you
never stopped loving you
even when you stopped loving Me.

I love you with a Father's love.
I care for you with a Father's care.
I delight in you with a Father's delight.
There is nothing I would not do for you.
Learn from your own experience with your children
     what it is to love with a Father's heart.

I am preparing not just a place for you to be with Me
    but I am preparing an eternity of joy for you
        an eternity of bliss!
Think of the most beautiful things your eyes have seen
     the most wonderful things your ears have heard
     the most enjoyable things that have been part of your
     life.

Those and far beyond those things
        I am preparing for you who love Me.[63]

I am preparing a thousand, a million, a trillion surprises
    for your eyes; for your ears;
    for all that is YOU because you love Me!
I not only desire your coming
    but I wish to create in you a longing to be with Me,
     your Father.

You are to be at home in your Father's heart.
He gives to His beloved, even as they sleep.
    If you find more and more sleep overtaking you
     as you come to be purified, rest in that sleep.
My strength is replacing all that is weakness in you.

Only as you are willing to lay down all the glory
that may follow you,
will you be able to enter into the fullness
of the glory of your Father.
Learn from Jesus how to give Me all the glory.
In glorifying your Father,
you will be glorifying Jesus.
When the time comes you will share in that glory.
But for now your task is to give **all the glory**
to your Father, to your Savior and to the Holy Spirit
and then indeed, you will live in My glory.

Jesus speaks plainly of the Father.
If you do not hear plainly
it is because you are not listening or
you are listening for something that isn't there.
The revelation of the Father is so simple
any child can receive it
although no one will ever fully comprehend it.

How do I love you?
I love you with an everlasting love
with a father and a mother's love from all eternity.
From your mother's womb I have called you by name. [64]
I love you with a forgiving love
a creative love
an effective love.
I love you not because of who you are
but because of who I called you to be
not for what you would make of yourself
but for what I would make of you
not because you never fail Me
but because even in those failures
I can redeem you and love you.

How do I love you?
I love you in every weak moment of your life.
I love you with a Father's love
    that called you forth into existence
        and holds you even now in the palm of My hand.
How do I love you?
I love you with the same love I have for Jesus.
    I cannot love you more than I do.
I have sent My only Son to die upon a cross for love of you.
I have sent the Spirit of love to live His life in you.
I love you with a love that is big enough to take in
        your whole family
        your neighborhood
        your church
        your city
        your nation
        all the nations.
I love you with a love that gave My only Son
    to bear your sickness and infirmity
        that you might be healed.
How do I love you?
I love you with an enabling love
    so that you can truly say to Me
    Father, I love you too!

Indeed, I am with you
    but you will never know the power of this "withness"
    unless you are also with Me.
With means to walk with
        to talk with
        to be with.
    Be with Me, as a child
        and I will be with you, as a Father.

Enter into My Presence
 that you may know Me as the Great I Am
                        the Absolute
                        the Irresistible
                        the Infinite
                        the Omnipresent
                        the Omniscient
                        the Omnipotent
                        the King of kings
                        the Lord of lords.
**When you truly come to know the Great I Am,
 you will come to know the Great You Are.**

13

MORE

Who are you to say, "Enough! Enough!" when I
your God say, "There is more! There is more!"

*No matter how much we have, we haven't got enough!
All of us have a giant-sized vacuum within us that needs to be
filled. God keeps enlarging our vessel. We need to constantly
get on the Potter's wheel so God can re-shape, re-fashion, re-
mold our vessel so we can hold MORE of His love, His truth,
His power . . . more of His divinity in our humanity.*

*When we say, "Your move, God!" He is there to fill
whoever is willing and waiting.*

Who are you to say, "Enough! Enough!"
when I, your God, say, "There is more! There is more!"
There is MORE I would reveal to you
MORE I would pour out upon you
for I am a God of surprises!
Eye has not seen nor ear heard
nor has it entered the heart of man
to dream what God has prepared for those who love Me.[65]
These are not idle words
I who spoke them will bring them to pass.
Come to know Me as a God of surprises even now!

You say, "God, You are too much!"
Yes, My child,
I am too much for your little mind.
So I will give you a new heart and a new mind[66]
that all I desire to give you
can be contained in that new heart and new mind.

My child,
You have hungered and thirsted
          for more of My life
          for more of My truth
          for more of My love.
You have sought Me in the day
          and you have sought Me in the night.
But I tell you I have hungered and thirsted for you
                    from all eternity with an infinite hunger
                              with an infinite thirst.

          If you ask, I will create in you
               a new hunger and
               a new thirst
               that I may satisfy it.

I would speak from the depths of your being.
I am more and more Lord of those depths
          for you are open more and more
               to a work I desire to do there.
It is a bulldozer work
          a delicate craftsman's work
               that I entrust to no other than to My hand.
It is a work that requires the total yielding of
                    your intellect
                    your past
                    your present
                    your future.
Know for certain that I,
               who hold the whole world in My hand,
          can surely hold your little world.
               without destroying or allowing ruin.
Trust Me like never before.
Yield to Me the nothingness you are
          and you will come to know the everything I am.

I am bringing about the reign of My Son in you.
That is why you find yourself more quiet
                        more at rest.
As His life takes over, I am more active;
        and you can be more passive.
This is a new thing for you, but it is not new for Me
                nor for the saints who are with Me.
It is not new for what I am doing across the face of the earth.
Trust the newness to Me.
        I hold you in My love.
            I will not let you fall for you are Mine.

I speak to you a word of GROWTH
                a
                    word
                        of
                            STRETCHING

                and
                    a
                        word
                            of
                                CHANGE.
THERE IS MORE FOR YOU!
        MORE of My way that I would show you
        MORE of My truth that I would teach you
        MORE of My life that I would empower you to live.

I have called you
>and you have been faithful to that call.
But today I call you to a greater faithfulness
>in speaking My Word
>in putting on My thoughts
>in using My gifts
>in being My witness.
Not only do I call you to this
>but I empower you for this.

That you may be empowered—LET GO!
Let go of all that is sin, bitterness, resentment, and
>hopelessness in your life.
Let go of all that is idol, superstition, witchcraft, or
>work of darkness from your past.
Let go of the scars of your own sins
>and the sins of others against you.
I see the situations you are in
>that you are powerless
>>to change.
>>>Give them to Me.
I see the circumstances
>that block your hope.
>>>Give them to Me.

>>I will smash down the iron walls.
>>I will break the chains that bind you.
>I will loose the Lazarus-cloths that keep you bound.
There is nothing I will not do that you may grow.
There is nothing I cannot do that you may grow.
Put together your willingness and My power and you will see
>growth!
>>>Growth in yourself!
>>>Growth in your family!
>>Alone I will not . . . Alone you cannot.

Together we can do whatever needs to be done.
Together we can plant whatever needs to be planted.
I am so ready to build My Kingdom.
But I need you to be a living stone.
>   I need your heart willing to grow and change.
>   I need your mind willing to be taught and stretched.
>   I need your hands willing to reach out with My power.
>   I need your lips willing to speak My words.
>   I need your will to say "Yes" not only to what I am doing
>   *but to the way I would do it.*
Yield yourself to Me
>   your plan to My plan.
>   All I have already spoken
>   I confirm and I pledge to do.
You will be recreated and transformed
>   and I will be glorified in you
>   and you in Me!

14

SOVEREIGN MOVE

Do you realize how precious you are to the heart of God? How precious you are to the heart of your Savior?

*We need to take a long, serious look at the bad news
that will not go away, no matter what means we use to drown
it, to deny it; what TV channel we switch to, what magazine
or newspaper we read. It's there!*

*Today's challenge is: to rise above it, to cry out beyond
it for the Holy Spirit to teach, to touch, to heal us, our families, our nation, our industries, our churches.*

*We need the ultimate surrender of ALL as we pray a
final—* "Your Move, God."

Do you realize how precious you are to the heart of your
    God?
                         how precious you are to the heart of your
                         Savior?
By the power of My Spirit I call you today, to a realization
    of your preciousness in Our sight.
Only as you realize how precious you are
    will you be ready to believe what I am ready to do for
       you.
Look around you and see who it is that I call precious
    that you too, may reverence your brother and your
       sister.
Look within you and see what it is that I call precious
    that you may reverence the vessel that I have made you.
Look above you and praise your God for His magnificent
    goodness
    and marvelous mercy in your life.
Even as I call you, My child, I call all of My people
    to celebrate My goodness
    to celebrate My mercy
    to celebrate My omnipotent power in your midst.

Lift up your voices
   lift up your hearts
      lift up your lives in a mighty shout of praise
         worship and thanksgiving!
For I have made you who you are.
   I have brought you where you are.
   I have formed you into a precious people for My service
         and for My praise.

Yes, I have worked mightily within you!
   And I will do an even mightier work among you
   for the time is short
   and the enemy would sift you and have you.
      He has done it and he plans to do it
      to wage an all-out attack on My work among you.

And I have done it and I plan to do it
      to wage an all-out attack on his work among you!
For this I have summoned forth My angelic forces.
For this I will gift you as a people and as a church
      with gifts and power you do not have.
For I see your hungering and your thirsting.
   I see your emptiness and your brokenness.
   I see your weaknesses and your despairings.
   I see your need for deliverance and for healing.
With infinite compassion I see the roots of your bondages
         your weaknesses
         and your sicknesses.
I see needs among you much bigger than you are
   hunger much vaster than you can imagine
   heart-cries for a Savior everywhere.
I ask you to see in the HEART of your God
   a HUNGER to satisfy your hunger
   a LOVE to satisfy your lack of love
   a WORD sent forth to do whatever needs to be done.

The task is so big you have said: "What is the use?"
The work is so hopeless, you have given up hope.
The power needed so limitless, your hands have fallen limp.
　　　But I say to you today: TAKE COURAGE for I, your
　　　　　God,
　　　am not discouraged by the enormity of the task
　　　and I will not be defeated or thwarted
　　　by the strength or strategies of the enemy.
　　　ALL POWER IS MINE IN HEAVEN AND ON EARTH!
　　　As it is Mine I give it to you.
　　　Power will not be lacking for the work I call you to do.
But you must make it yours today.
　　　Tomorrow is too late.
　　　　　Tomorrow may never come.

You are facing dark times and dangerous times.
　　　They will only be dark
　　　if you do not look to your God to be your light.
　　　　　They will only be dangerous
　　　　　if you do not stand in Our victory.
Right now many of you stand before Me
　　　as immature in the ways of following your God
　　　　　immature in the effectiveness of your ministry
　　　　　immature in the vision of what I am doing in your
　　　　　　　midst.
Many of you are still ruled by your personal whims and
　　　fancies.
But I say to you this day
if you will say yes to the sovereign move of My Spirit
over you and among you
　　　I will mature you this day even as I matured the Apostles
　　　in that Upper Room to speak when there are those
　　　　　　　　　against you
　　　　　　　　　to live a life of selfless service
　　　　　　　　　to teach as you have never taught
　　　　　　　　　to preach as you have never
　　　　　　　　　　　preached.

I will follow your words with signs and wonders
like you have never seen.
But you must intercede for Me to do this.
You must believe for Me to do this today
for yourself and for each other.

I desire My people to be a Spirit-filled people
filled with a new FULLNESS of MY LIFE, MY LIGHT,
and MY LOVE.
I desire you to be a Spirit-led people
led by a new directness as I gift you with ears to listen to
Me.
I desire you to be a Spirit-empowered people
empowered by a new power that totally matches your need
and My resources.

You shall see in your spirit this day a new awakening
   that will bring you into a new vision of the Majesty of your
      God
         a vision not only of My tenderness, My love, and My
            mercy but
         also of My justice, My holiness, and My wrath.
Like Peter and Isaiah, I give you a vision of the sinfulness of sin
                                             and the holiness of
                                                your God.
As I do I call you to a constant and deeper repentance
                        and a constant and deeper joy in your
                           salvation.
Not only do I call you to a deeper joy in your salvation
   but I call you to share this joy
      in a mission of evangelization of the world.
No one of you can say that you are too small
                                 too uneducated
                                 too unimportant
                                 too unhealed
                             or too ungifted.
I call you to begin as you are
   in the spirit and calling of a John the Baptist
      right where you are in your home, your neighborhood,
         your church.
Go means GO. Preach means PREACH. Good news means the
   GOOD NEWS—
            The Father loves you.
            Your Savior died for you.
            The Spirit is available for you.
You will speak with authority if you look to Me and heed My
   voice.

I give you My compassionate love for the poor, the unwanted
                                 the deprived
                                 and the depressed.

138

I give you MY LOVE to destroy the hatred
                              and the bitterness that is
                              destroying them.

That you may be a people of power I will pour forth in a new
    way
    all that is gift and fruit of the Spirit in your life.
For not by might, not by power, but by My Spirit shall all
    these things be done. [67]
I will bring you individually and as a body
    into a renewed dependence on My Spirit.
        He will teach you, quicken you, strengthen you
            convict you, heal you, and give you liberty
                to live as a child of a king and
                    to come to the throne of your Father.
        He will give you discernment and direction that will be
            pure gift.
        He will reveal to you what it is that I am doing and
                              what it is that I would have you to
                              do.
        He will teach you to use the sword of the Word
                    and to answer the enemy with My Word.
        He will bring you into an experience of your Father's
            love.
YIELD your poverty, your sinfulness, your whole self
    to the sovereignty of your God. Admit your need. Confess
    and repent.
Cry out your willingness to OBEY,
                              to WALK WITH ME
                              to LISTEN TO MY VOICE
                              to KEEP YOUR EYES FIXED ON
                              ME
                              to ALLOW THE SOVEREIGN
                              MOVE OF MY SPIRIT.

139

My child,
You cannot understand it.
    It is too big for your little mind.
But I ask you to believe that your Father
    desires to work with infinite love
                and infinite power.

You are about to see
    the Age of the Father's Love.
In the past there were mighty revivals
    that moved across the face of the earth
            through which hundreds of thousands of people
            came into the Kingdom.
Today millions are being taught and touched by God.
The sovereign power of God is ready to move far beyond
    the power of any revival with might and power
        that is ready to touch peoples
                            families
                            churches
                            cities
                and nations.
Your God is ready to renew and restore the face of the earth.
In Me is power enough
    to dispel all the darkness on the face of the earth.
In Me is love enough
        to cast out all the hatred of the whole world
            and to bring about a Kingdom of total peace and love.

My child,
You are powerful to Me when you open your mouth
    and you are powerful when you close your mouth.
You are powerful in renewing My church
        simply and purely
    because of the relationship I have with you.
Hold this and treasure it above all things
    for without that depth, that beauty, that power
        all your words will be as chaff
        your comings and goings as nothing.
Hold up your relationship with Me
    that I may deepen it and intensify it.
        I will be as effective in you
        as you will allow Me
        to be Father to you.
    to hold you, to embrace you, to love you.
Let this be your emphasis:
    to be more and more fully My child
    to be more and more fully the beloved of My Son
    to rejoice more and more fully in My choice of you.
Rejoice in Me. Glory in Me!
    Then indeed I will use you
        mouth open or closed
            traveling or at home.
I will use you for the coming of My Kingdom
    for the renewal of My church.

Child, there are moments like now
    when you see to a greater degree your stupidity
        your slowness to comprehend
        your inability to flow with My Spirit.

Have I not been speaking to you for weeks about resting?
But you had all your own ideas
    all your own ways in which you would like Me to work.
You were about your strivings
                your contrivings
                your figuring out
                and denying yourself things
        that you might have enjoyed, if you had not been so
            tied up
            with doing your own thing as well as My thing.
    And have you not only today
            seen the vision of why I call you to rest?
Now you see how simple it could have been.
You see your Father in a new light.
You see Me as your Sovereign Lord
        really able to achieve what I said I would achieve
            to do what I said I would do
                to bring about the Kingdom
                    in ways you never dreamed!

POSTSCRIPT

I would like to share with you three Scriptures the Lord gave me when I was lacking the faith and courage to go on to bring this writing where it is today.

"Oh that my words were written!
Oh that they were inscribed in a book!
That with an iron stylus and lead
They were engraved in the rock forever" (Job 19:23-24).

"Thus says the Lord, the God of Israel, 'Write all the words which I have spoken to you in a book' " (Jer. 30:2).

And finally when I was under that last cloud of doubt:

"And He said, 'The God of our fathers has appointed you to know His will, and to see the Righteous One, and to hear an utterance from His mouth.'
'For you will be a witness for Him to all people of what you have seen and heard' "(Acts 22:14).

FOOTNOTES

Because of the spontaneous nature of prophetic word the Scriptures in this writing are mostly paraphrase. The following list of Scriptural references is given for your convenience for further thought and prayer.

1. Matt. 11:25
2. Ps. 50:10
3. Wisdom 11:22
4. Isa. 57:13
5. John 14:10
6. Isa. 48:18
7. Col. 1:12-13
8. Matt. 5:18
9. Luke 6:20
10. Luke 12:32
11. Phil. 3:8
12. Rom. 12:2
13. Luke 10:24
14. Col. 1:13-14
15. Phil. 4:19
16. Song of Sol. 2:12
17. Ps. 37:4
18. Isa. 1:18
19. Luke 1:45
20. Rev. 22:17
21. Song of Sol. 3:4
22. Ps. 97:5-6
23. Zeph. 3:17
24. Phil. 3:17
25. II Cor. 10:5
26. Rev. 12:10
27. Isa. 6:6
28. Isa. 49:16
29. Matt. 18:3
30. Eph. 1:4
31. John 14:10
32. II Cor. 1:19
33. Matt. 11:12
34. John 17:21
35. Rom. 2:4-5
36. I Sam. 3:9
37. Luke 11:9
38. II Cor. 10:5
39. Eph. 3:20
40. Heb. 4:12
41. Matt. 24:35
42. Isa. 30:21
43. Zeph. 3:17
44. Eph. 5:8
45. Ps. 91:11
46. Zech. 4:6
47. I Peter 5:8
48. Isa. 4:4
49. Gen. 22:14
50. Luke 1:46-49
51. Ps. 103:12
52. Ps. 139
53. John 15:1-4
54. Luke 23:42
55. Ezek. 22:30
56. Luke 15:25
57. II Cor. 5:17
58. John 15:4
59. Rev. 1:8
60. Luke 22:19
61. I John 2:16
62. Eph. 1:4
63. I Cor. 2:9
64. Isa. 49:1
65. Isa. 64:3
66. Ezek. 36:26
67. Zech. 4:6